Wild Flowers
of Spain

by

CLIVE INNES

COCKATRICE PUBLISHING LTD
Whitchurch, Hampshire, England

First published 1987
by Cockatrice Publishing Ltd.
Whitchurch, Hampshire RG28 7LN

British Library Cataloguing in Publication Data
Innes, Clive
  Wild Flowers of Spain
  1. Wild Flowers — Spain
  I. Title
  582' .13'0946   QK329

ISBN   1   870353   01   3.

Photographs by the author and Joan Flack

Printed in England

INTRODUCTION

Considerable interest has been expressed following the publication of the first of this series earlier this year. Such interest certainly encourages the continuation of these booklets – No. 3 is already well under-way for publication in 1987.

Spain is particularly fortunate in its vast array of native plant-life. A number of very authoritative books have been published on the plants of Europe, and these bear record to the almost endless species which can be discovered within Spain by the enthusiastic plantsman. With but little effort beautiful plants and flowers can be seen on every hand – on the high mountain slopes and hillsides – in lowland scrub country – and along, often in very close proximity to, the coastal regions both north and south.

It would appear, however, that a great number of plants have received no 'visual' mention – inasmuch as no colour photographs have been published to allow for easier recognition and identification. It is hoped that these booklets will help to provide this service.

Brief descriptions are given of each of the species illustrated, also a broad outline of the particular habitats. Botanical nomenclature is used, together with the appropriate common-name where applicable.

For the host of people who have taken up residence in Spain, and for the many thousands who flock to this country throughout the year, it is hoped this booklet will be another contribution to their pleasure. Why not explore the countryside more? It is in very easy reach of any city, town or village!

Clive Innes

ACACIA dealbata Link.   (Leguminosae)

Common name – *Silver Wattle – Mimosa*

Among the many Australian trees which have been introduced and become naturalised in many parts of Southern Spain is the well-known Mimosa – and indeed this is considered one of the most outstanding. A fast-growing species which can reach 10-12m high – very decorative and colourful, and especially in evidence throughout the Mediterranean region.

It has a smooth greyish-brownish trunk and spreading, leafy greyish-white branches. Leaves are bluish-green in colour, compound, divided firstly into several 'sections' which again are divided into 30 or more feathery leaflets, each about 2mm long. Flowers are mainly terminally borne – these in branched clusters of small rounded heads of bright yellow, which are scented, principally from the ends of the branches.

Flowering is from April to early June.

ACACIA longifolia (Andr.) Willd.   (Leguminosae)

Common name – *White Sallow*

This is one of several Australian trees which have become naturalised and indeed flourish in southern Spain – and although originally intended for ornamental purposes, is also used in sandy places for the purpose of stabilizing the soil. The branches have the capability of rooting whenever they are buried in the sand. They are most frequently to be found along the Mediterranean coastal regions.

A colourful and most decorative tree, which can grow to 9m high. The leaves are long-linear or narrow-oblanceolate – very like those of the willow – to 15cm long, dark-green or greyish-green in colour and leathery. Flowers are small, globose and a bright sulphur-yellow, densely packed together in stalkless cylindrical spikes 3-5cm long, emerging from the axils of the leaves. The seed pods which follow are about 10-15cm long, twisted and curved.

Flowering principally in March and April.

ALLIUM flavum L.   (Alliaceae)

Common name – *Yellow Onion*

This is a variable species and certain forms have botanical recognition such as *A. flavum* var. *minus* Boiss., a more dwarf variety. It is found in many parts of the country, from north to south at altitudes to nearly 3000m – usually in meadows or woodlands – frequently encountered in the Pyrenees.

A bulbous plant with smooth, channelled, somewhat cylindrical grey-green leaves 1-2mm thick, these sheathing the flowering stem towards the base. Flowers are borne in a loose umbel at the apex of a stem to about 30cm tall. Few or several flowers form the umbel, each long-stalked, bright yellow in colour – the umbel subtended by 2 long papery bracts – the uppermost flowers stand upright, whilst the surrounding ones curve downwards. The long projecting stamens are a feature.

Flowering is from June to late August – the leaves preceding flowers.

ALLIUM triquetrum L.   (Alliaceae)

Common name – *Triquetrous Garlic*

One of the most attractive of the ornamental onions which has
become naturalised in many parts of Europe, including U.K. It is
to be seen in moist places – in shady woods, often near streams in
southerly parts of Spain, from low levels to altitudes of about
1000m.

Flower stems vary from about 15-35cm tall – they are three-cor-
nered, a feature noted by the specific title – *triquetrus* meaning 3-ang-
led. Leaves are broadly linear with a sharp keel below – 5-12mm
wide and 30cm long. Flowers are large, pure white bell-shaped, with
a green central stripe externally on each petal, these are each about
1-1.5cm long. As many as 5-15 flowers form the graceful 1-sided
loose umbel, each flower rather inclined to be pendulous.

Flowers are at their best from March until late June, and in general
are long-lasting. It is sometimes called the '3-cornered Leek'.

ANTHYLLIS montana L.   (Leguminosae)

Common name – *Kidney Vetch*

A low-growing, mat-forming species which is to be discovered in rocky areas in the Sierras in southern Spain including the Pyrenees, and it is quite widely distributed, usually in rocky or very stony areas.

Stems are rather soft and almost or entirely leafless, arising from the very woody base of the plant. Leaves are sparsely arranged, carried on short or longish stalks – decidedly pinnate and hairy, divided into 8-15 pairs of slender leaflets, each leaflet 5-10mm long, the top central leaflet more rounded. Flowers are borne on short stems in rounded terminal clusters of either purple or pinkish pea-shaped blooms, very densely arranged, and each cluster surrounded by two deeply-cut leaf-like bracts.

Flowering period is more or less limited to June and July, after which the typically pea-like pods appear.

ANTHYLLIS tetraphylla L.   (Leguminosae)

Common name – *Bladder Wort*

This is also known as *Physanthyllis tetraphylla* (L.) Boiss. A very low-growing spreading and creeping annual which gets its common name because of the swollen calyx, a feature which distinguishes this from other species within the genus – and this becomes increasingly larger until it is almost globular in shape when in fruit. It is readily encountered in grassy places in southern Spain, at high and low levels.

It is a greyish-green, soft hairy plant with compound leaves having 3-5 rounded leaflets, the upper one always longer, larger and wider than the others. Flowers are small, pale yellow and generally tipped with orange or red, formed in quite dense clusters of 3-6 individual flowers which are stalkless. The globular reddish fruits have two seeds only.

Flowering period extends from March to July.

ASTRAGALUS monspessulanus L. (Leguminosae)

Common name – *False Vetch or Milk Vetch*

This is a densely bushy, low growing plant, slightly hairy and very free-flowering. It is usually associated with limestone country – on dry hillsides or meadows – in rocky, stony ground on mountainous terrain in the south, east and central Sierras of Spain at altitudes from 400-2500m or more.

Leaves are pinnate – these being divided into 10-20 rounded or oblong blunt leaflets, deep-green in colour. Flowers are more or less terminal and form an attractive inflorescence being a rich reddish-purple or purplish-violet – very occasionally a white form can be found and these are about 2cm long – they are in quite compact oval stalkless clusters and are carried on stems which arise directly from the rootstock. Slightly curved hairy fruits follow, these 3-4cm long, typically pea-like in shape.

Flowers can be seen from mid-April to well into August.

CAKILE maritima Scop. (Cruciferae)

Common name – *Sea Rocket*

This is a member of the Cress family – an interesting rather than an attractive species. A rather scrambling, spreading plant generally lodged in rocks or stones and growing in the sand along the Mediterranean coastline – almost at high tide level.

The stems can reach 30-60cm in length, and, like the foliage, are quite succulent and fleshy. Leaves are soft with very distinctive oblong lobes, and generally the leaves are only few in number. Flowers variable – pink, pale-purplish, rarely white – and quite sweetly scented, borne terminally on longish stems. The fruits are another interesting feature – these are in two unequal parts or sections – the lower part conical, the upper 'mitre'-shaped.

It has been proved to be rather an irregular flowering species – but they do develop at any time between June and late September, often earlier or later.

CENTAURIUM erythraea Rafin.   (Gentianaceae)

Common name – *Common Centaury*

This is one of those choice little plants which often needs to be sought-after as so often it becomes swamped by other vegetation. There are two subspecies – *grandiflorum* (Biv.) Meld. and *majus* (Hoffm. & Link.) Meld., both of which have larger flowers than the species and also differing in other minor characters. It is widespread in the south of Spain, growing in grasslands and scrub, especially in the Mediterranean area.

An erect, slender plant, regularly branched with smooth stems – these are sparsely leafy – the main foliage being in the form of a basal rosette of linear pale-green, rather oval leaves. Flowers are carried in a loose cluster at the tips of the stems – varying shades of pink – the petals widely spreading – each flower 5-6mm across.

A very neat plant which flowers freely from June to late August or into September.

CICHORIUM intybus L. (Compositae)

Common name – *Chicory*

This is an erect or semi-sprawling perennial found in many parts of Spain, especially in the south of the country where it frequents dry stony places, often where there is limestone – at low to middle altitudes. The dried roots of this species provide the chicory of commerce.

A most variable species with stiff, hard stems of dull green – widely spreading branches and can grow from 30cm to 1m tall. The slender lanceolate basal leaves are deeply serrated, whilst those on the stems can be sparsely toothed or as is mostly the case, entire, and the undersides are covered with minute bristly hairs. The flowers are set along the branches, stalkless, 2-4cm across, varying colour-wise from deep-blue to pale-blue, sometimes even white or pink forms are found.

Flowers can be seen almost incessantly from May to August, and quite frequently much later in the year.

CLEMATIS recta L.   (Ranunculaceae)

Common name – *Bushy Clematis*

This is but one of the several Clematis species to be found wild in Spain – it seems to frequent dry hillsides in shaded areas and hedges, perhaps in the south more than elsewhere, principally at altitudes from about 200-600m.

It is an herbaceous perennial without the climbing habit! It has hollow stems and branches, these to well over 1m in height – it is however, rather a 'soft' species with the branches trailing and spreading in all directions. Leaves are pinnate with 5-7 deep-green oval leaflets, 2.5-6.5cm long. Flowers in terminal clusters, white, scented – each flower about 2cm wide – the margins of the petals being minutely hairy.

This densely bushy plant creates a spectacular display when in full bloom from late June through to early September – but this might vary according to habitat.

CONVOLVULUS althaeoides L.   (Convolvulaceae)

Common name – *Mallow-leaved Bindweed*

This is a sprawling or clambering perennial species which can be located in scrub or bushy regions on hillsides or low country, even to sea-level. Most frequent in central Spain and along the Mediterranean coast.

Stems are slender and hairy and these can become well over 1m in length. The leaves are oblong-cordate, especially the lower ones – the upper ones deeply divided into 5-9 unequal slender segments the central one being longer – and all are minutely silky-hairy, deep-green in colour – and in shape certainly meriting its common title. Flowers are funnel-shaped, 3-4cm or more long, deep rich pink in colour, borne solitary or in pairs on long stalks from the leaf-axils.

Flowering period is from late April to July, although this may vary slightly according to location.

CRITHMUM maritimum L.   (Umbelliferae)

Common name – *Rock Samphire*

This is a coastal plant which can rightfully be described as a succulent species. A rather bushy plant with a hard, gnarled rootstock which anchors in rocky crevices along the coast-line, obviously benefiting from the sea-spray. It is very prevalent along the Mediterranean shores.

A very fleshy species with stems 20-50cm long, slightly grooved and terete, occasionally short-branching. Leaves greyish-green – glossy and smooth, somewhat tripinnate with fleshy leaflets, 2.5-5cm long and about 6mm wide. Flowers are pale-yellowish, sometimes greenish-white, about 2mm across and borne in quite large umbels of 10-15 or more individual 'rays' at the terminal ends of the stems.

An interesting plant which is in flower from July through to early November, after which it tends to produce seeds in profusion.

CROCUS vernus Hill   (Iridaceae)
    . subsp. **albiflorus** (Kit. ex Schultes) Asch. & Graeb.

Common name – *Purple Crocus*

The common name certainly contradicts the flower colour depicted. The fact is, it is a most variable species with a range of colours including rose-pink, shades of purple – and white. A widespread species – in Central Europe and elsewhere – and in the Spanish Pyrenees the white form is to be found.

The rootstock is a tunicated corm from which both leaves and flowers arise. The foliage is generally apparent at flowering time, but the leaves continue growing after the flower has fully opened. Flowers are pure white – sometimes lightly feathered with purplish-blue at the base of the outer segments – the style and stamens a rich orange, often the stamens almost white.

It flowers in February and March at altitudes of about 2500m in meadows and on grassy slopes – also on more gravelly terrain.

DAPHNE laureola L.   (Thymelaeaceae)
subsp. **philippi** (Gren.) Rouy.

Common name – *Spurge Laurel*

This a rather low growing shrub which, with age, develops quite a
thickish stem and a few spreading, equally thick branches. It has a
fairly restricted habitat on low and higher slopes in the Pyrenees of
northern Spain.

It rarely exceeds 60-75cm in height and invariably develops almost
horizontal branches. Leaves are a deep green with an almost wavy
surface, oblong in shape and quite leathery – and these are carried
towards the ends of the branches. Flowers are yellowish or greenish-
yellow about 6mm long and narrowly bell-shaped, slightly scented,
and formed in small clusters mostly towards the tips of the branches.
After flowering, the fruits quickly form, these being small black
berries.

Flowers can be seen from late February to April.

ECBALLIUM elaterium (L.) Rich.   (Cucurbitaceae)

Common name – *Squirting Cucumber*

A fleshy, spreading species with thick sprawling stems, which is found chiefly near the sea, but also on rough wasteland throughout the Mediterranean region. The seeds are reputedly poisonous – but apparently the rootstock contains an ingredient said to be useful in alleviating rheumatism and other ailments.

Stems are thick, coarse and fleshy and can spread and grow to over 50cm long. Leaves are rough, somewhat triangular in shape, sparsely toothed, dark-green, but whitish on the underside. Flowers can be either male or female, long stalked, bell-shaped – the males usually in small clusters, the females solitary – small and coloured pale yellow. Fruits are 4-5cm long – broadly cylindrical in shape, green and very hairy. These will explode at a touch, so care must be taken to prevent the dispersing seeds reaching the eyes!

Flowering and fruiting continues from late March until early October.

ECHINOPS ritro L.   (Compositae)

Common name – *Globe Thistle*

This is a perennial plant often attaining 1m in height – attractive with its spiny rounded terminal heads, whether in flower or not. It is found in many parts of Spain, on low to high ground in rocky, dry uncultivated places, perhaps more abundant near to the Mediterranean region.

Stems are generally branched, more or less erect – each branch carrying a spherical head about 3m across which can produce either blue or whitish flowers, each head subtended by several slender blue bracts. Leaves are basal or sparsely set along the branches – bright-green on the upper surface, and white cottony on the underside – very tough and deeply cut into several narrow, sharply spined tips. A feature of the species is the slender white cottony felt on the stems as well as the foliage.

Flowering time is between July and September.

ERICA multiflora L.   (Ericaceae)

Common name – *Western Mediterranean Heath*

A colourful shrub with woody stems and branches and densely leaved – reaching to about 1m in height and a spread of 60cm or more. It is a plant which is particularly common in the north, central and south of Spain on hills and low country, mainly in wooded areas.

As a young plant the stems are pinkish-green, but gradually over a period of 2-3 years becoming very woody. Leaves slender and a matter of 1cm or so long, greyish-green and grooved on the underside, arranged in whorls. Flowers develop in clusters of few or many – each bloom rather bell-shaped, about 5mm long – carried on a very fine stalk, pale pink, the style and anthers protruding well beyond the tips of the petals.

Flowering can be variable according to habitat, but generally from late July to November.

GLADIOLUS communis L.   (Iridaceae)

Common name – *Purple Gladiola*

This is one of the few species of Gladiolus native to Europe, all of which are to be found in Spain. Several specific titles have been ascribed to this plant, and even now, perhaps, there is doubt as to which name has precedence. It is found mostly in the Mediterranean region – on grassy hillsides and pastures, often spreading to stony uncultivated places.

A cormous plant which carries a stem 50cm or more long, with basal green or red sheaths which are prominently veined. Flowers are formed in a 1-sided spike of 10-20 individual blooms of rose-pink to purplish-red, the segments 3-4.5cm long, only the central upper one being slightly longer, each flower subtended by a shorter bract. It is usual to find the lower segments lined with white or deep red. There are varieties recorded, differing only little from the type.

Flowering is from April through to early July.

GLADIOLUS illyricus Koch   (Iridaceae)

Common name – *The painted Gladiolus*

This probably gets its common name because of the prominent white 'brush' marks on the lower segments, certainly more obvious than the markings on *G. communis* L. This has a very wide distribution, extending from the Mediterranean region of Spain through to the Middle East. Very often it can be discovered in moist scrub areas at lower altitudes, more rarely in open fields.

Stems vary from 25-50cm tall, a few leaves sheathing the base which are narrowly sword-like to about 5-9mm wide. The spike is 3-10 flowered, slender, erect with a few axillary branches. Flowers are deep pink to almost purple to 4cm long, with shorter sub-tending bracts. The upper flower segments unequal – the upper central being longer than the laterals – the lower three about equal with a central white streak.

Flowering occurs from early April to June in the Mediterranean region.

GLOBULARIA alypum L.   (Globulariaceae)

Common name – *Shrubby Globularia*

This is an evergreen perennial – a much-branched, spindly low-growing shrub and very common in dry scrub areas and rocky terrain from north to south Spain, and very prevalent along the Mediterranean coastline.

It frequently reaches 50-60cm high, rather lax branches which are very brittle. Leaves are lanceolate, leathery and short spiny tipped – often the margins with small sharp teeth. Flowers are borne terminally – globular heads of about 2cm wide consisting of numerous small lilac-blue flowers – the head subtended by hairy brownish bracts. Each flower more or less cylindrical with a single 3-lobed lip, and they are sweetly scented.

Plants are mainly winter flowering – from late September to March, although this much depends upon habitat. It is reported to have medicinal qualities.

GYNANDRIRIS sisyrinchium (L.) Parl.   (Iridaceae)

Common name – *Barbary Nut*

This very attractive, miniature member of the Iris family is a really choice little plant, the flowers of which only open after midday and are faded by the following morning. It is found throughout the Mediterranean region – on hillsides or in clearings within wooded areas. It was for long known as *Iris sisyrinchium* – a title still accepted by many.

A cormous species, the corm said to taste of nuts – hence the common name. Leaves are slender and channelled, rather rush-like, straight or widely spreading and longer than the flowering stem. Stems 3-10cm long, occasionally longer carrying flowers in groups of 2-4 from the axils of the papery bracts. Flowers 3-4cm diameter, varying shades of blue with white or yellow markings in the centre, but no beard on the falls.

Flowering is from March to May, rarely to the end of June.

HELICHRYSUM foetidum (L.) Moench.　　　　(Compositae)

Common name – *Stinking Everlasting*

The common name is not too complimentary, but undoubtedly this species is strong smelling! A tall perennial species gradually developing almost bushy proportions , to about 1m in height. A native plant of South Africa which has been introduced into parts of Europe and become naturalised in the south of Spain. It is found growing in rocky, stony ground on hillsides close to the Mediterranean coastline.

A sturdy species with greyish-green leaves set at intervals along and clasping the felted stems, very white-woolly on the under surface. The bright yellow flower heads are carried terminally, larger than those of *H. stoechas* – rounded firstly, then opening and spreading to about 2cm across with many papery, shiny yellowish or whitish involucral bracts.

This can be discovered in flower between early May to late July.

HEPATICA nobilis Miller (Ranunculaceae)
Common name – *Hepatica*

This anemone-like plant is perhaps better-known as *H. triloba* or even *Anemone hepatica*. It is a very low growing species and much associated with mountainous areas of Spain, particularly the Pyrenees and some of the high Sierras of the central and southerly regions – found in grassy meadows, in woods or scrub or limestone rocky places.

The leaves are all basal – 3-lobed with distinct veining, dull-green on the upper surface, purplish beneath and carried on rather slender fleshy stalks. Flowers are terminally borne on stems arising direct from the rootstock – these are 1.5-2.5cm wide, in shades of colour from pale-pink to purple, rarely white – each subtended by 3 leaf-like green bracts.

A charming miniature which can be seen in flower between March and May.

IRIS lutescens Lam. (Iridaceae)

Common name – *Dwarf Iris*

Perhaps this is better known as *I. chamaeiris*, a title which continues to persist! It has a rhizomatous rootstock and eventual growth is to about 30cm high when in bloom. There are several forms – the variety found on the rocky hillsides of south-easterly and northerly Spain have either purplish or yellowish flowers. They are not high altitude plants, rather at fairly low levels, often in sparsely wooded areas, or dry stony places.

Leaves are pale green in colour, about 30cm long, 2.5cm broad, sword-shaped and partially recurved. Stems are 1-2 flowered – each flower 6-7cm across with a perianth tube of 2-3cm in length – these carried on the stem, proper, of 5-18cm long. Whatever the flower colour, the beard on the outspread 'falls' is whitish or orange-yellow.

Flowering is from early March to early May, often earlier and later.

IRIS pumila L.   (Iridaceae)

Common name – *Pygmy Iris*

One of the smallest species of the genus, but being somewhat variable is often difficult to determine. A rhizomatous plant which occurs in many parts of Europe but can also be located on fairly high
ground in the south-east and east of Spain growing in low scrub and
bush-covered country.

Flower colours vary a great deal – and whilst the bluish-purple form
seems to dominate in Spanish habitats, yellow or whitish flowers are
recorded in other areas. Leaves are glaucous-green, sword-shaped,
slightly curved backwards. Flowers are stalkless or nearly so. The
5-6cm diameter flower has just about 1cm of stalk below the 5-10cm
long perianth tube – so the impression is given of a far longer stem.
The outer segments – the 'falls' – are recurved and have creamy-
white or yellow beards.

Flowers are at their best in March and through to early May.

IRIS xiphium L. (Iridaceae)

Common name – *Spanish Iris*

This well-known bulbous Iris has helped to win lasting and permanent recognition of the beauty of the Spanish flora. It grows in fields, hills and low mountains of southern districts, particularly in moist areas together with species of *Aquilegia*.

A tall growing plant reaching 40-60cm high when in flower. Leaves precede the flowers – these are linear and channelled, 30-50cm long. Stems are erect, usually carrying a single head of flowers with rather swollen bracts. Flowers are violet-purple or bluish, about 10cm diameter – the falls have a somewhat rounded blade and a fiddle-shaped haft, widely spreading with a conspicuous yellowish-orange patch reaching to almost the tip of the blade. The standards more or less erect.

There are varieties of this species, differing in colouration or size of flower, but all flowering from April through to June.

KNAUTIA arvensis (L.) Coulter   (Dispacaceae)

Common name – *Field Scabious*

This is one of a few species comprising a genus closely related to the better known Scabious. Fairly erect but slender plants which are widespread in many parts of Spain, particularly prevalent in the south where they are found on waysides, in scrub and dry grassy places.

Stems are slender, 30-45cm tall, almost leafless – the leaves right at the base of the plants are more or less entire, whilst those on the lower part of the stems are partially lobed. Flowers are terminally borne in the form of a circular head of numerous pale bluish flowers – the head being about 3cm across – the small individual flowers around the circumference of the head are longer than those in the centre.

The flowering period is from May to late September, although this can be variable.

LILIUM martagon L. (Liliaceae)

Common name – *Martagon Lily or Turk's Cap Lily*

This elegant but variable lily is very well known in cultivation, and certainly retains its elegance in its own habitat. The distribution is widespread, and is found growing in pastures or wooded areas in the Pyrenees of eastern Spain.

A bulbous species which develops flowering stems from 60-90cm or more in the wild. Leaves are arranged more or less in whorls of 4-10 at intervals along the stems. The flowers are beautiful, slightly pendent – the outer petals recurved to show the rich pinkish-purple or whitish of the inner surface – the underside has swellings of a deeper shade. However, flower colourings can vary, from pinkish-orange to almost yellow – likewise stems can be shorter or longer – this very much depending upon habitat conditions, which are invariably calcareous.

Flowering at their best during June and July.

LINUM perenne L. (Linaceae)

Common name – *Perennial Flax*

This very beautiful and spectacular species is quite a variable plant – and there are varieties or subspecies recorded, differing mainly on account of flower size. It is widespread in many parts of central and south Spain, especially the Pyrenees at altitudes of about 1600m in dry grassy places.

A woody based perennial with stems to 60cm tall, these being 'loosely' erect. Leaves are stiff, linear to narrowly-lanceolate about 2.5cm long and 2.5mm wide, 1-veined and set alternate along the stems – somewhat glaucous-green in colour. Flowers are 1.8-2.5cm across, pale to bright blue carried on very straight stalks, and borne terminally in branched panicles – occasionally white flowers are in evidence. Petals are somewhat oval in shape with rather papery edges.

Flowering from May to August.

LONICERA etrusca Santi   (Caprifoliaceae)

Common name – *Mediterranean Honeysuckle*

This is a deciduous honeysuckle of climbing and spreading habit which is located only in limestone areas. It is, however, readily found in the south of Spain, frequenting wooded or scrub terrain and hedges, especially in the Mediterranean region at altitudes to about 400m.

Plants can climb and scramble to 4m or more, with many elongated branches. Leaves are leathery, 3-8cm long, oval in shape, the upper ones encircling the stem. Flowers creamy-yellow and generally suffused a delicate pink, borne in small clusters on stalks about 4cm long – always in groups of 3 with 3-4 groups forming the cluster. They are elusively scented. Fruits follow and these are in the form of red oval berries which contain but few seeds.

Flowering at their best from May to early August, but very often flowers occur until early September.

MALVA sylvestris L. (Malvaceae)

Common name – *Common Malva*

A colourful perennial or biennial species which has become established in many parts of Europe, including Britain. It is, however, seen to best advantage in its Spanish habitats along the Mediterannean coast – in low-lying wooded areas and waysides, frequently becoming almost a nuisance in more developed parts.

It is a robust plant – erect or semi-erect – with hairy stems and branches. The leaf-shape helps determine the species – they are more or less rounded with 5-7 distinct lobes, and these lobes are toothed. Flowers are 3-4cm across – the widely spreading petals of rich-purple are striped with a deeper shade and the tips are prominently indented, the sepals are much shorter than the petals and very hairy on the under-surface. Usually two flowers are borne together.

Flowering is primarily from May to early September.

MUSCARI altanticum Boiss. & Reut.   (Lilaceae)

Common name – *Grape Hyacinth*

A fairly common bulbous species which can be found throughout much of Spain, and for that matter, elsewhere in Europe. It is particularly in evidence in the south of the country – on hillsides to 2000m altitudes, in fields and stony places, where it frequently abounds in 'colonies'.

The leaves appear before the flowers – these are very slender, almost grass-like with a distinct groove from tip to base, and invariably lying flat on the ground. Stems vary in length from 10-30cm and carry a terminal head of dark-blue flowers 3-4cm long, each of the 10 or more individual blooms about 4mm long and oval in shape. There is also a form of this known as *M. atlanticum* var. *neglectum* which is similar except that the leaves are wider, and the little flowers slightly longer, more bell-shaped with white 'teeth'.

Flowering from February to late May.

NARCISSUS requienii M.J. Roemer   (Amaryllidaceae)

Common name – *Rush-leaved Narcissus*

This is a species known by other names such as *N. juncifolius* and is very similar to *N. jonquilla*. A graceful plant which is found in the south and south-east of Spain, particularly on the slopes of the Pyrenees at about 500m altitude and frequently occurring at similar elevations through to near Jaén in the Sierra Morena.

A bulbous plant which needs little introduction. It has rush-like leaves of deep-green only 1-2mm wide. Flowers are borne terminally on slender stems – usually 2 or more in a cluster – sweetly scented – deep yellow spreading petals and a small cup-shaped trumpet. On the slopes of Bernia, above Calpe in Alicante Province a few colonies of plants can be seen – they are certainly more abundant in Sierra Morena.

Flowering can be variable according to habitat, but mainly from late March to early May.

NARCISSUS serotinus L.   (Amaryllidaceae)

Common name – *Autumn Narcissus*

This little plant could easily be overlooked as belonging to this popular genus – it is so very different. The habitat is very widespread, being found on both sides of the Mediterranean, and the Balearics. In the south of Spain it grows in rocky areas and dry hillsides at about 150m altitude down to almost sea-level along the Mediterranean coastline.

A slender, delicate species with very thin, thread-like leaves which usually develop after the flowers. Flowering stems are from 15-25cm tall.and bear a single terminal flower about 2-3cm across – this is pure white in colour with a very small yellow trumpet and a long greenish tube, and they are fragrant. The perianth tube is long and slender scarcely ever widening.

The flowering period is during September and October, although in some areas this extends well into November.

NERIUM oleander L.   (Apocynaceae)

Common name – *Oleander*

This well-known plant requires very little description, although un-fortunately it fails to be hardy in Britain. It is variable – flowers can vary from the normal pink to deeper shades. Sometimes white or creamy-white flowers are in evidence – that shown above was seen in a dry-river bed near Jalon, Alicante Province. Right along the Mediterranean it is possible to find Oleanders growing in dried-up watercourses, moist ravines and the like, usually not too distant from the sea.

Large shrubby plants – sometimes forming thickets to 3-4m high. Leaves are greyish-green, narrow and pointed, 10-20cm long, in whorls along the branches. Flowers are borne in few-flowered clus-ters at the tips of the branches – each flower 3-5cm diameter – the pink form certainly dominates the scene! Fruits are cylindrical con-taining many 'tufted' seeds. Flowers are at their best from April through to September.

OPHRYS tenthredinifera Willd.   (Orchidaceae)

Common name – *Sawfly Orchid*

This very distinguished little orchid is found at quite low altitudes in the south of Spain – in sparsely wooded areas, often in quite stony ground – more abundant from Alicante Province through to Almeria and towards Malaga, where it has seemed to flourish on quite open grassy places.

A very erect orchid with stem up to 30cm tall bearing 3-8 flowers. A multi-coloured flower with pale to deep-pink sepals which have a green median line, very broad and almost rounded. The petals are smaller and also pink. The lip is the outstanding feature – this is somewhat 'fan'-shaped with 2-lobes which are edged around with yellow or greenish-yellow with a central reddish-maroon area margined with white and blue – the whole lip is quite hairy.

Flowering from mid-February until the end of May, dependent upon location.

41

ORCHIS purpurea Hudson　　　　　　　　　(Orchidaceae)

Common name – *Lady Orchid*

This choice but variable orchid, also called the Dark-winged Orchid, is native of many parts of Europe, including Britain, parts of Asia and North Africa. It grows in calcareous soil in woodlands and scrub and grassy places, especially in the south of Spain, also in sheltered areas of the lower Pyrenees in the north.

A sturdy species 20-40cm or more tall – the unspotted leaves are in the form of a bright green rosette – only 3-6 quite broad leaves to a rosette. Flowers are in a dense terminal spike – fragrant – but varying colour-wide. The purple or maroon-red hood is 1-1.4cm long, this comprised of the petals and sepals – the 3-lobed lip is either pink, violet or white and prominently spotted – 2 slender 'arm' like lobes and a lower broader one divided into a further 2 lobes with a minute 'tooth' between. The spur is short and downward pointing.

Flowering from March to May.

OROBANCHE crenata Forsk.   (Orobanchaceae)

Common name – *Bean Broomrape*

An unusual plant which is parasitic on species of the Leguminosae, particularly *Vicia* and *Lathyrus* – also known to be a menace to cultivated crops of beans and peas. It is widespread throughout much of Spain, and in particular the region bordering the Mediterranean. The host plants can frequent woodlands, fields and waysides, often on very dry, calcareous ground.

Flowers are borne on quite a sturdy, erect stem – these are formed into a dense spike of orchid-like flowers – varying in colour from white to yellow and veined with pinkish-red or purple – each about 3cm long. The lip of the flower is divided into 3 unequal lobes, the central one being the largest. An interesting feature is the fact that the flowers are scented.

Flowering throughout March to late June, but the dried "inflorescence" can last for several weeks later.

43

PALLENSIS spinosa (L.)   (Compositae)

Common name – *Pallensis*

This is also known as *Asteriscus spinosus*. An erect, regular branching plant which grows to nearly 1m tall. It is found in abundance in the south of Spain, generally at low levels, in stony and uncultivated ground and fields.

The leaves differ – those at the base are broadly oblong and narrowing to the stalk – the upper ones more or less lance-shaped, stalkless, and clasping the stem. The flower head consists of numerous florets of dull yellow arranged in two rows – each head about 2cm or more across. This is subtended by large star-like bracts, very stiff and spine-tipped, extending horizontally almost star-like to well beyond the flowering head. The inner bracts are papery and hairy, oval in shape.

Flowering from late March to early August, depending upon location.

PARONYCHIA argentea Lam.   (Caryophyllaceae)

Common name – *Silvery Paronychia*

A very low spreading species which is readily distinguished by its very silvery appearance. It is particularly prevalent in the south of the country in the Mediterranean region, in dry rocky parts at low altitudes.

This is a perennial plant with many trailing and spreading slender branches – the lanceolate leaves about 1.5cm long have long silvery stipules and are set in pairs along the branches – the margins are minutely hairy. Flowers are arranged in fairly dense clusters appearing towards the tips of the branches – they are green and individually very small and almost overwhelmed by a covering of very conspicuous silvery bracts which are longer than the flowers. The five sepals are somewhat papery – narrow and pointed.

The flowering period can be variable, but mainly from April to June.

PHLOMIS lychnitis L. (Labiatae)

Common name – *Small Jerusalem Sage*

This closely resembles *P. fruticosa* L. from which it can be determined because of its shorter growth and more whorls of flowers. It is widespread in central and southern parts of the country, on calcareous soil in dry stony places, and sparsely wooded areas especially near the Mediterranean coastline.

A shrubby plant of erect growth, 45-60cm tall – the stems are white felted and unbranched. Leaves narrowly elliptic, greyish, rough on the upper surface and white-felted below. Flowers bright yellow arranged in 4-8 whorls at intervals along the stems – 6 to 10 flowers to a whorl – each flower about 2.5cm long, 2-lipped and silky-hairy – each whorl subtended by long, silky-haired bracts, which have a wide base narrowing to a pointed tip.

Flowering season is mainly from May to July, but this can vary according to location.

PHLOMIS purpurea L.   (Labiatae)

Common name – *Purple Jerusalem Sage*

A tall-growing species, sometimes to nearly 2m tall but generally
60-90cm and it is to be found in many parts of central, eastern and
southern Spain where it frequents dry hillsides, in rocky and stony
places, generally at low to medium altitudes. The similar *P. herbavent* L.
has more flowers to a whorl.

This very erect multi-stemmed plant is distinguished by the oval-lanceolate leaves which are minutely hairy on the upper surface and
white-felted beneath, rough and leathery. New growth is always
densely covered with whitish "wool". Flowers are pinkish-purple or
deeper purple and arranged in whorls at intervals along the felted
stems, 5-8 flowers to each whorl – each flower to about 2.5cm long
– just below each whorl are soft greyish silky bracts, narrowly lance-
shaped or elliptic.

Flowering from late March to late May.

47

PISTACIA lentiscus L.   (Anacardiaceae)

Common name – *Mastic Tree*

This is an attractive evergreen shrub which can attain 2-3m high, becoming almost tree-like. It is found in many parts of Spain and widely distributed throughout the Mediterranean region, very abundant on low hilly country and in the *maquis*. It is a worthy representative of a genus which includes *Pistacia vera* noted for its pistachio nuts!

A densely branched and spreading species, often almost tree-like, with aromatic pinnate leaves of deep-green each with 3-6 pairs of leathery leaflets, broadly lanceolate with blunted tips and there is no terminal leaflet. Flowers are very small, reddish, with red anthers – in dense erect clusters from the leaf axils. The fruits which follow are globular, 5-6mm across, at first red then becoming black. The resin extracted from the stems is the mastic used for making varnish.

Flowering from April to June.

PRUNELLA hyssopifolia L.   (Labiatae)

Common name – *Self Heal*

This very interesting and quite colourful plant is fairly low-growing and is perennial. It occurs principally in limestone areas of central and eastern parts of Spain, and more especially in the Pyrenees, also occurring in S. France.

It is a stiff and quite erect species, the stems smooth but sometimes coated with short bristly hairs. Leaves are without stalks (a particular characteristic), narrowly lanceolate and entire. Flowers are borne in quite dense clusters at the tips of the stems – violet or pinkish-violet in colour, very rarely white, each flower 1.5-2cm long – as many as 12-20 or even more forming a very attractive cluster, each cluster subtended by leaves. This differs from the more common *P. grandiflora,* a species sometimes seen in cultivation, which has no subtended leaves to the flowers.

Plants are summer flowering from May to September.

49

PRUNUS communis (L.) Fritsch.   (Rosaceae)
  var. **dulcis** (Miller) D.A. Webb

  Common name – *Almond*

One of the most fascinating scenes along the Mediterranean region are the Almond Trees in full blossom in February and March. There are varieties of the species – *P. communis* var. *dulcis* (Miller) D.A. Webb is the one usually seen and this produces the sweet almonds of Valencia fame. There is also *P. communis* var. *amara* which is less interesting.

Trees reach anything from 5-10m – the green branches clothed with lance-shaped, coarsely-toothed, slightly rough leaves. Flowers are generally pink, although white flowers are frequently to be seen, and are about 3-5cm across, these appearing before the leaves along much of the upper parts of the branches.

The wrinkled nut is contained within the tough rough-coated leathery, green fruit, which usually ripens in late summer.

PSORALEA bituminosa L.   (Leguminosae)

Common name – *Pitch Vetch*

This is so-named because of the leaves smelling of tar when they are crushed. It is something of an untidy plant, its soft, sometimes stiffish, branches spreading in all directions. It frequents the Mediterranean region especially in south-western areas, in dry stony places and low scrub-covered terrain.

It is quite sparsely branched – a perennial – often gowing to about 1m in height. The leaves are trifoliate and these bedeck the slender branches along their lengths – those leaflets towards the base of the stems are sometimes almost rounded whilst those near the tips are slender and pointed. Flowers are similar to those of clover, each about 1-1.5cm long, borne in terminal, rounded heads on very long stalks – lilac-blue or bluish-violet – 10-15 individual flowers to each cluster.

Flowering from April to July.

RESEDA alba L.   (Resedaceae)

Common name – *Upright Mignonette*

There are some 17 species of this genus, most of which are to be found in Spain. This is a very erect, almost bushy plant, which quickly captures the eye, made all the more spectacular because of the many flowered spikes. It occurs primarily in the south along the Mediterranean coastline, but can also be seen near the Galician coast, in sandy dunes or on rocky hillsides.

Plants attain 45cm or more high. Leaves are deeply cut into several narrow lobes with undulating margins. Flowering stems are slender and upright, densely covered with small white flowers, each about 9mm across, the petals distinctly 3-lobed, surrounding 10-12 prominent yellow stamens. Small seed pods develop later, each about 1cm or little more long, and they carry 4 small 'teeth'.

The flowering season can be most variable – probably seen at their best from March to May.

SALICORNIA europaea L.   (Chenopodiaceae)

Common name – *Glasswort*

This is but one of a number of "Glasswort" species generally referred to as *Halophytes* and represented within a few genera which are native of the saltflats of Spain, these plants having been able to adapt their growth to saline conditions. This species is the only European member of a comparatively small genus and can be located in mud-flats and salt-steppes in the Province of Malaga and Almeria.

A very low shrubby plant – which might well be determined a 'succulent' – the stems are fleshy, somewhat swollen, and jointed – and, if trodden on, will crackle underfoot. They have no leaves. The flowers are in a terminal spike looking as if composed of small clusters – these are groups of rose-pink flowers almost embedded in the joints of the stem – only the central flower of each group being obvious!

An unusual plant of which little has been recorded. It is in flower during the summer months.

SAXIFRAGA mèdia Gouan   (Saxifragaceae)

Common name – *Reddish Saxifrage*

This is a low-growing perennial which forms slightly elongated rosette-tufts of leaves. It is not unknown in cultivation, and is, in fact, quite a popular rockery plant. Its habitat is quite widespread in the Pyrenees – and can be discovered in the eastern mountains of Spain, growing in calcareous rocky terrain, often at over 2000m altitudes.

The leaves are greyish-green in colour, broad and sharply pointed, leathery, about 2cm long, narrowly oblong, formed into rosettes, the bases of which are pink. The flowering stems are about 8-10cm high, covered with fine reddish hairs. The pink or pinkish-purple flowers are carried in loose but quite dense panicles – the flowers are only just visible as they emerge from the bell-shaped calyces, which are red and hairy.

Flowering from June to August.

SCILLA bifolia L. (Liliaceae)

Common name – *Alpine Squill*

This rather fascinating little bulbous plant is not unknown in cultivation. It is found in low as well as in mountainous country of north, central and western parts of Spain – frequenting woodlands and shaded fields at altitudes of over 1500m.

It has a particular feature – two broad shiny leaves – a fact recognised in the specific title although it is not unknown for more leaves to form! The leaves are broadly lance-shaped, but wider towards the tips, grooved and outward curving from about halfway up the 10-20cm long stem. Flowers are in loose, one-sided clusters of 2-8, widely spreading, bright-blue to purplish-blue in colour, each about 1-1.5cm long, without bracts – the anthers a deeper shade, almost violet-blue. Flowers of pink or white can occasionally be seen.

Flowering from February through to August, but this is likely to vary according to habitat.

SCILLA peruviana L.   (Liliaceae)

Common name – *Peruvian Squill*

The title does not describe its habitat – it has no association whatsoever with Peru or any other S. American country. It is a large bulbous plant, more or less evergreen and is native of southern Europe and North Africa – and can be found in moist areas along the Mediterranean coast.

It is a short to medium-sized plant having 4 to 8, rarely more broad strap-shaped, spreading leaves of shiny deep-green, about 4-6cm wide. Stems stout and fleshy, 20-40cm tall bearing a terminal flattish or pyramid-shaped head, 12-15cm across. This consists of numerous pale or violet-blue flowers – each flower 1-2cm long, star-like, carried on a short stalk 3-9cm long. There is also a very attractive white form, possibly a mutation which has been seen in the Malaga Province.

Flowering from April to early July.

SEDUM album L. (Crassulaceae)

Common name – *White Stonecrop*

A new generic title has been recognised for this species and should be recorded as *Oreosedum album* (L.) Grulich. This very variable small succulent plant has been known in cultivation for many years. It has many habitats throughout Europe, Asia and North Africa and is quite common in most mountainous and rocky regions of Spain – usually in rock crevices and the like.

A stoloniferous evergreen plant, rarely exceeding 8cm high but vigorously spreading. The green stems are slender, frequently branching and covered with fleshy rounded or elliptic leaves set alternate along their lengths. Leaves are shades of green, often turning pinkish or brownish-red during periods of very dry weather, especially if in full sun. The inflorescence is many-flowered borne terminally on the stems – each flower 6-9mm wide – white, sometimes slightly suffused pale pink. Flowering May to mid-September, but often appearing earlier and later.

SENECIO doronicum (L.) L.   (Compositae)

Common name – *Chamois Ragwort*

This erect, rather greyish plant is quite variable, and there are 2-3 botanical varieties recognised. The habitat is fairly widespread, especially in mountainous regions from the Pyrenees to the Sierra Nevada, in rocky stony ground or on grasslands at altitudes to about 3000m.

Stems are fairly short and erect, 30-50cm tall and covered with minute hairs. Leaves are elliptic to oval-lanceolate, thick and leathery, toothed along the margins, greyish-green above, white felted below – those leaves towards the upper part of the stem are much narrower, and clasping. Flowers are golden-yellow, 3.5-5cm wide, solitary or 2-3 together, each with 15-20 ray florets. The involucre bears another row of long bracts.

Flowering period is from June to August, often later in the more southerly regions.

STAEHELINA dubia L   (Compositae)
Common name – *Tassel Flower*

This is one of the more unusual species within this family of vastly differing plants, its shape justifying its common name. It is fairly widespread on the Iberian Peninsular, especially in the south, central and eastern parts of Spain invariably on very dry stony ground at both high and low altitudes.

A perennial woody-based, bushy plant with erect or semi-erect branches, all white-felted. Leaves are very slender, deep-green, minutely white hairy on the under-surface – the margins mostly serrated, sometimes entire, 3-5mm wide. Flowers are borne at the tips of the branches – an almost cylindrical head about 3cm long and 3-5mm wide. of purplish-pink flowers and apical tufts of whitish, slightly bristly hairs. The involucral bracts are covered with whitish hairs suffused with purple.

Flowering from about May through to August.

THYMELAEA hirsuta (L.) Endl.   (Thymelaeceae)

Common name – *Fleshy-Leaved Thymelaea*

This most unusual shrubby plant which can attain 1m in height is found right along the Mediterranean coastline – very often on cliff sides or on rocky and sandy places, rarely at any great distance from the sea – it is particularly in evidence in the provinces of Alicante and Malaga.

The branches are quite tough and elongated and somewhat white felted, covered almost completely with small, overlapping oval, scale like leaves of deep green, these looking just as if they were swollen. Flowers are yellow with hairy petals, about 5mm long, several together forming clusters at intervals along the stems. The leaves rarely exceed 5mm long and 2mm wide – the lower surface being covered with silky-cottony white hairs.

They are in flower from late September through till May – almost continually.

TULIPA australis Link.   (Liliaceae)

Common name – *Southern Tulip*

This wild tulip should better be known as *T. sylvestris* subsp. *australis*. This is just one of very few tulips native of Spain – this and *T. celsiana* are very similar, varying chiefly on the stem height and the flowering period. It is found on the mountains and hillsides or in grassy places near to the Mediterranean mostly in rough country and rocky areas.

This little bulbous plant generally has only two leaves – glaucous-green, quite narrow and grooved. The stem in from 15-20cm long, sturdy and erect. The small flowers are bright yellow with the outer segments flushed reddish or pinkish externally – all segments are about 3cm or so long, slender, pointed, the anthers about 4mm long, slightly scented and they gradually open wide in full sun. Flowers are borne terminally and solitary and last several days.

Flowering from April to July.

UMBILICUS rupestris (Salis.) Dandy   (Crassulaceae)
    var. **truncatus** (Wolley-Dod) Rowl.

Common name – *Pennywort*

A common succulent species which occurs throughout much of Europe including Britain. It is a variable plant and there are botanical varieties recorded. It can be found right around the Mediterranean region at altitudes to about 500-600m on cliff sides, rock crevices and similar places – very widespread on the high ground in Alicante Province.

It has a tuberous rootstock from which arise almost circular fresh-green succulent leaves – 2.7cm wide, prominently depressed near the centre and truncate or cordate at the base – at first forming a low rosette, then loosely spreading on fleshy stems. Flowers are borne on a tall many-flowered spike 30-40cm high, greenish or pinkish in colour – each flower to about 1cm long and slightly drooping.

Flowering from late April to July.

INDEX